ILLUMINATIONS

FROM THE

BHAGAVAD-GĪTĀ

ILLUMINATIONS
FROM THE
BHAGAVAD-GĪTA

By Kim & Chris Murray

MANDALA
publishing group

San Francisco   Eugene   Singapore   Mumbai

Mandala Publishing Group
103 Thomason Lane
Eugene, OR 97404
phone: 800 688 2218
fax: 541 461 3478
mandala@mandala.org
www.mandala.org

1585-A Folsom Street
San Francisco, CA 94103
phone: 415 626 1080
fax: 415 626 1510

239C Joo Chiat Road
Singapore 427496
phone: 65 342 3117
fax: 65 342 3115

ISBN 1-886069-21-2

Printed in China through Palace Press International

Contents

Foreword   vii

Preface   ix

Introduction   xiii

The Illuminations   1

Notes   77

Foreword

eep within the forest comes the sweet sound of a flute. Like a tiny bird alighting on the smallest branch, the gentle music weaves a melody. And I am healed of care and woe. And I am soothed from constant thoughts of "me" and "mine". What is this sound? The "I" that "thinks" is mesmerized into a pleasant calm. My footsteps lead me where no path has been. Peacocks calling in the canopy. All creation bows to this sweet sound. Time stands still. The forest sighs. There within the deepest glade the blue child stands. Govinda! Garlanded, jeweled with crystal flowers. How His eyes they gaze upon all form. How His transcendental being glows, like a halo for the world to see. In Him I am free.

I write a spontaneous poem as I look at this wonderful work, *Illuminations From the Bhagavad-Gita,* by Kim and Chris Murray. How apt the title. To "illuminate" the wisdom from ancient Vedic literature. An inspiration for humanity today. Chris has selected the classic verses and brought his extensive knowledge of Indian art to this beautiful book. Kim, with her deeply emotional painting, has brought forth an exquisite vision of the Deity at play in our midst. We are enriched!

–Donovan   1998

Preface

bhagavad-gita is like the sun, shining for everyone. It is not a sectarian doctrine, meant for a particular faith or class of people. It is the Song of God, meant for the enlightenment of us all. *Bhagavad-gita* is the essence of all Vedic literature. "Veda" means knowledge, and Lord Krishna, the original knower of the Vedas, is the author of *Bhagavad-gita*. By studying this transcendental literature we are learning from Krishna himself. Krishna declares in the *Gita* that "he who studies this sacred conversation worships Me by his intelligence."

Though first spoken long ago, *Bhagavad-gita* remains utterly vital today. It is not sentimental but is practical — a handbook of wisdom for our troubled times. Arjuna was experiencing many difficulties on the Battlefield of Kurukshetra. Today, we are likewise burdened with many serious problems. War, poverty, pollution and greed are everywhere, and getting worse. This is an age of anxiety. But the heart of the Lord is mercy and, in *Bhagavad-gita*, Krishna gives us the knowledge by which our activities may be purified and our suffering mitigated. If a person is interested in increasing his own happiness and that of society at large, the *Gita* can show the way. Krishna spoke *Bhagavad-gita* to take us from the darkness of ignorance to the light of knowledge—to illuminate us.

This book is a celebration of the glory of *Bhagavad-gita* and its author, Lord Krishna. Presented is a selection of verses from the *Gita* (which one should read in its entirety to fully relish its sublime philosophy) and a series of illustrations depicting some of Krishna's wonderful pastimes and activities.

Krishna's nature is transcendent. He is the Supreme Beauty who resides in everyone's heart. His form is all attractive and unlimited. In the spiritual world, love rules supreme. It is by love and devotion that Krishna may be known. This is the natural function of the soul. In such spirit, this book is offered to Krishna and to his intimate devotee, His Divine Grace A.C. Bhaktivedanta Swami Prabhupada, and his followers. If this book gives them some transcendental pleasure, then our efforts are a success.

–Kim and Chris Murray

Introduction

he time is five thousand years ago. The scene is a battlefield at Kurukshetra, India. A chariot bearing charioteer and archer sits between the opposing phalanxes of two mighty armies.

The battle which is about to begin is the inevitable climax of years of political intrigue. It is a fratricidal war to determine who will occupy the throne: righteous Yudhisthira, who is the eldest son of the dead King Pandu and the rightful heir, or his treacherous cousin, Duryodhana, who is trying to usurp the kingdom. Conchshells, bugles, and drums sound as two huge military forces poise for battle. From his chariot between the armies, the archer, Arjuna, beholds the soldiers on the enemy's side – many of whom are his own relatives – and he becomes overwhelmed with compassion and familial affection. Weeping, he lays down his weapons and refuses to fight.

At this point *Bhagavad-gita* begins. Arjuna humbles himself before his chariot driver, who we learn is no ordinary charioteer but the Supreme Personality of Godhead Himself, Lord Krishna. Accepting Lord Krishna as his spiritual master, Arjuna asks for help in his moment of crisis, and for one hour the world stands still as the Lord instructs Arjuna, and subsequently all mankind, in the wisdom of *Bhagavad-gita*, the Song of God.

> *The Supreme Lord said: While speaking learned words, you are mourning for what is not worthy of grief. Those who are wise lament neither for the living nor the dead. Never was there a time when I did not exist, nor you, nor all these kings; nor in the future shall any of us cease to be.*

Thus a momentous dialogue ensues as Lord Krishna explains the science of the spiritual soul, the material nature, and the Supreme Personality of Godhead, who controls both the spiritual and the material. Lord Krishna says: "I shall now declare to you in full this knowledge both phenomenal and noumenal, by knowing which there shall remain nothing further to be known."

Today, fifty centuries later, *Bhagavad-gita* remains the world's most complete book of scientific spiritual knowledge. Within India's great treasure house of human understanding, the Vedic literature, *Bhagavad-gita* is perennially the most popular book. In the West, the *Gita* has had profound influence on philosophy and literature and has been studied by virtually all of our major thinkers for the past two hundred years.

The present volume, *Illuminations From the Bhagavad-gita*, is appropriately titled, since the *Gita's* teachings are indeed illuminating. As one verse says: "When one is enlightened with the knowledge by which nescience is destroyed, then his knowledge reveals everything, as the sun lights up everything in the daytime."

That these verse translations are taken from *Bhagavad-gita As It Is* by His Divine Grace A.C. Bhaktivedanta Swami Prabhupada, makes the book doubly illuminating. A shroud of mystical jargon, which is nothing more than imprecise, impersonal rhetoric, obscures most English translations of the *Gita*, but here the translations are refreshingly lucid – illuminating. The reader comes away enriched with the wisdom of *Bhagavad-gita*, not puzzled by riddles. These illuminations, designed and painted by Kim and Chris Murray, wed tastefully with each verse, as page after page radiates with the wisdom and beauty of *Bhagavad-gita*.

Far more than just a picture book, these rich pages illumine many of the *Gita's* eternal truths. Here are a few of them.

The soul is eternal:

> *For the soul there is never birth nor death. Nor, having once been, does he ever cease to be. He is unborn, eternal, ever-existing, undying and primeval. He is not slain when the body is slain.*

The soul is our permanent identity throughout this lifetime, and at death we transmigrate to another body:

> *As the embodied soul continually passes, in this body, from boyhood to youth to old age, the soul similarly passes into another body at death. The self-realized soul is not bewildered by such a change.*

Lord Krishna is the father of all souls, the source of creation, and the all-powerful controller:

Of all that is material and all that is spiritual in this world, know for certain that I am both its origin and dissolution.

I am the generating seed of all existences. There is no being — moving or unmoving — that can exist without Me.

Lord Krishna's immanence can be perceived throughout His creation:

Know that all beautiful, glorious, and mighty creations spring from but a spark of My splendor.

Lord Krishna, as the Supersoul, accompanies each transmigrating soul from one body to another:

The Supreme Lord is situated in everyone's heart, and is directing the wanderings of all living entities.

Lord Krishna enlightens His worshippers from within their hearts:

Out of compassion for them (the constantly devoted souls), I, dwelling within their hearts, destroy with the shining lamp of knowledge the darkness born of ignorance.

He also enlightens these devoted souls from without through His representative, the spiritual master:

Just try to learn the truth by approaching a spiritual master. Inquire from him submissively and render service unto him. The self-realized soul can impart knowledge unto you because he has seen the truth.

Lord Krishna, although immanent, is simultaneously situated transcendentally in the spiritual world of bliss and knowledge. And the transmigrating soul, after having been perfectly enlightened by Lord Krishna (the Supersoul), the spiritual master, and *Bhagavad-gita*, can also return to the spiritual world:

One who knows the transcendental nature of My appearance and activities does not, upon leaving the body, take his birth again in this material world, but attains My eternal abode.

—Satsvarupa dasa Goswami

You cannot see Me with your present eyes. Therefore I give you divine eyes, so that you can behold My mystic opulence.

Bhagavad-Gita 11-8

Illuminations
from
The Bhagavad-gītā
As It Is

DEDICATION

TO

His Divine Grace

A.C. Bhaktivedanta Swami Prabhupāda

The greatest exponent of the Bhagavad-gita and its teachings in the western world.

NEVER WAS THERE A TIME WHEN DID NOT EXIST, NOR YOU, NOR ALL THESE KINGS; NOR IN THE FUTURE SHALL ANY OF US CEASE TO BE.

As the embodied soul
continually passes,
in this body,
from boyhood to youth
to old age,
the soul similarly passes
into another body
at death.

The self realized soul
is not bewildered
by such a change.

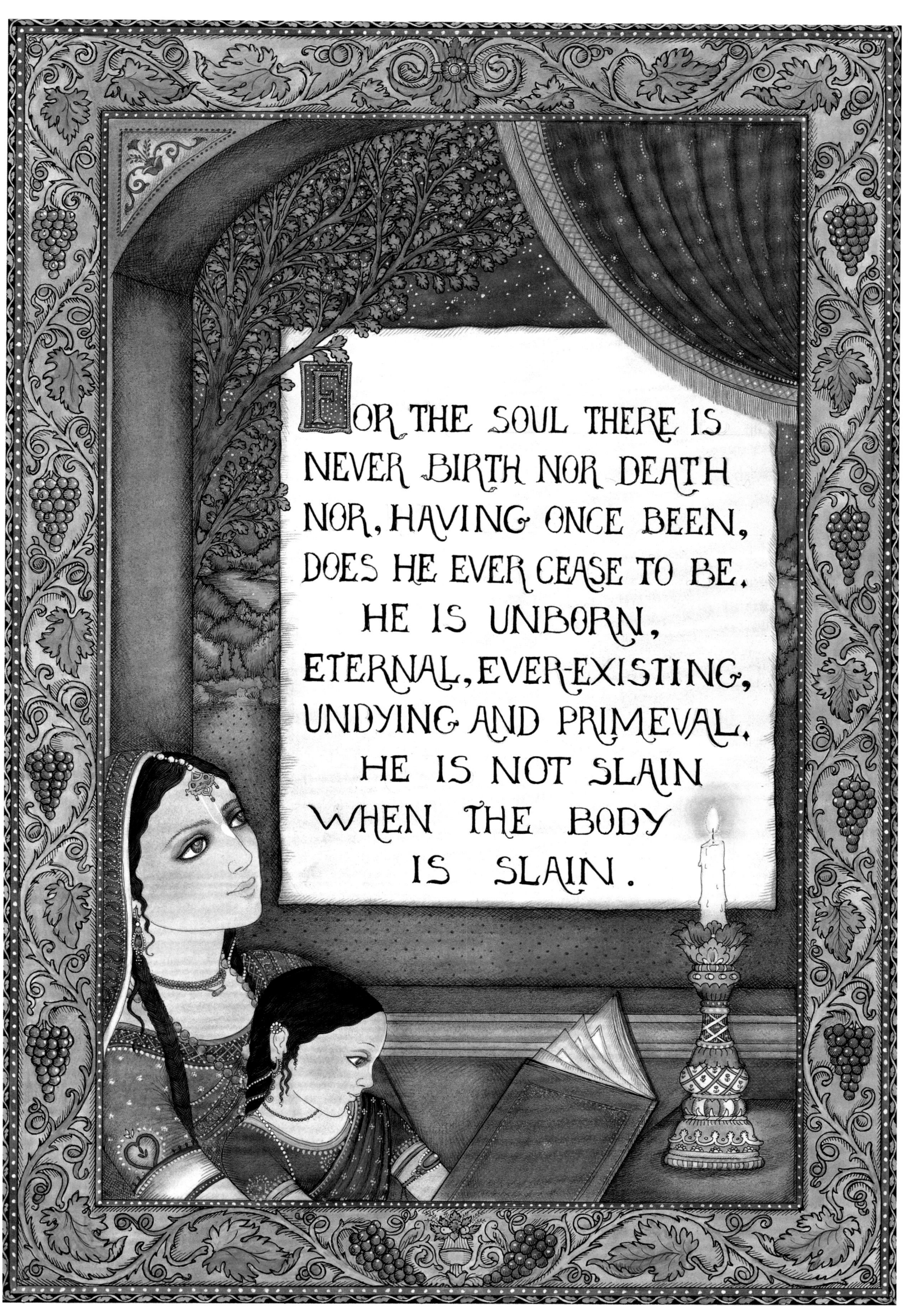

FOR THE SOUL THERE IS NEVER BIRTH NOR DEATH NOR, HAVING ONCE BEEN, DOES HE EVER CEASE TO BE. HE IS UNBORN, ETERNAL, EVER-EXISTING, UNDYING AND PRIMEVAL. HE IS NOT SLAIN WHEN THE BODY IS SLAIN.

FOR ONE WHO IS SITUATED
IN TRANSCENDENTAL CONSCIOUSNESS,
THE MISERIES OF MATERIAL LIFE
EXIST NO LONGER
IN SUCH A HAPPY STATE,
ONE'S INTELLIGENCE IS STEADY.
ONE WHO IS NOT IN
TRANSCENDENTAL CONSCIOUSNESS
CAN HAVE NEITHER
A CONTROLLED MIND
NOR STEADY INTELLIGENCE,
WITHOUT WHICH THERE IS NO
POSSIBILITY OF PEACE.
AND HOW CAN THERE BE
ANY HAPPINESS
WITHOUT PEACE?

Vṛndāyai tulasī-devyai priyāyai Keśavasya ca
Kṛṣṇa-bhakti-prade devi satyavatyai namo namaḥ

22

The Blessed Lord said; I instructed this imperishable science of yoga to the sun-god, Vivasvān, and Vivasvān instructed it to Manu, the father of mankind, and Manu in turn instructed it to Ikṣvāku.

That very ancient science of the relationship with the Supreme is today told by Me to you because you are My devotee as well as my friend; therefore you can understand the transcendental mystery of this science.

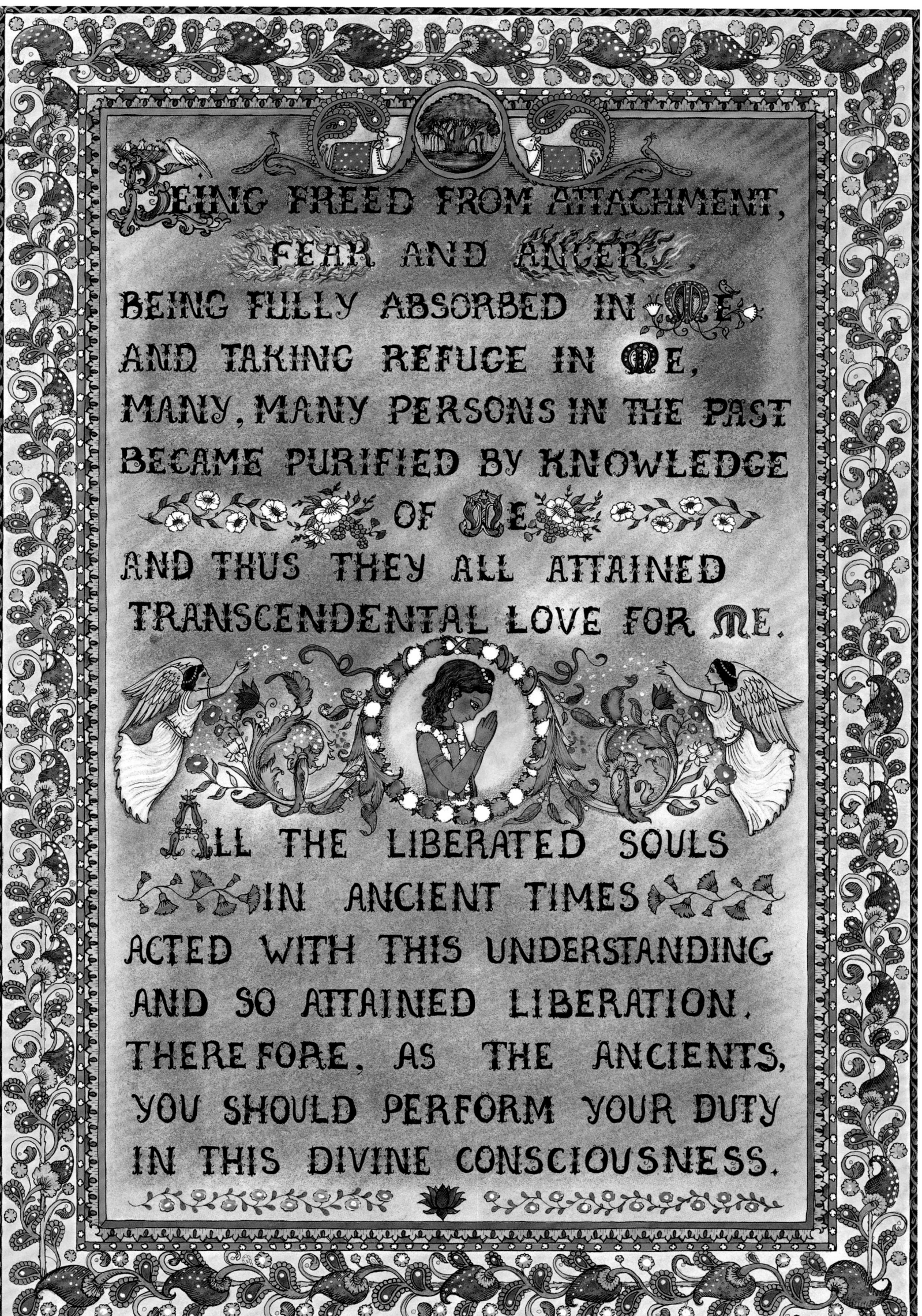

BEING FREED FROM ATTACHMENT, FEAR AND ANGER, BEING FULLY ABSORBED IN ME AND TAKING REFUGE IN ME, MANY, MANY PERSONS IN THE PAST BECAME PURIFIED BY KNOWLEDGE OF ME AND THUS THEY ALL ATTAINED TRANSCENDENTAL LOVE FOR ME.

ALL THE LIBERATED SOULS IN ANCIENT TIMES ACTED WITH THIS UNDERSTANDING AND SO ATTAINED LIBERATION. THEREFORE, AS THE ANCIENTS, YOU SHOULD PERFORM YOUR DUTY IN THIS DIVINE CONSCIOUSNESS.

JAYA JAGADISH HARE

JUST TRY TO LEARN THE TRUTH BY APPROACHING A SPIRITUAL MASTER. INQUIRE FROM HIM SUBMISSIVELY AND RENDER SERVICE UNTO HIM. THE SELF-REALIZED SOUL CAN IMPART KNOWLEDGE UNTO YOU BECAUSE HE HAS SEEN THE TRUTH.

Even if you are considered to be the most sinful of all sinners, when you are situated in the boat of transcendental knowledge, you will be able to cross over the ocean of miseries.

In this world, there is nothing so sublime and pure as transcendental knowledge. Such knowledge is the mature fruit of all mysticism. And one who has achieved this enjoys the self within himself in due course of time.

Govindam ādi-puruṣaṁ tam ahaṁ bhajāmi

One who works
in DEVOTION,
who is a pure soul,
and who controls
his mind and senses,
is dear to everyone,
and everyone is dear to him.
Though always working,
such a man
is never entangled.

When one is enlightened
with the knowledge
by which nescience is destroyed,
then his knowledge reveals
every thing,
as the sun lights up
every thing
in the day time

One whose happiness is within, who is active within, who rejoices within and is illumined within, is actually the perfect mystic. He is liberated in the Supreme, and ultimately he attains the Supreme.

A MAN MUST ELEVATE HIMSELF
BY HIS OWN MIND,
NOT DEGRADE HIMSELF,
THE MIND IS THE FRIEND
OF THE CONDITIONED SOUL,
AND HIS ENEMY AS WELL.

FOR ONE WHOSE MIND
IS UNBRIDLED,
SELF-REALIZATION IS
DIFFICULT WORK,
BUT HE WHOSE MIND IS
CONTROLLED AND WHO STRIVES
BY RIGHT MEANS
IS ASSURED OF SUCCESS.

IF ONE OFFERS ME WITH LOVE AND DEVOTION A LEAF, A FLOWER, FRUIT OR WATER WILL ACCEPT IT.

TO THOSE WHO ARE CONSTANTLY DEVOTED AND WORSHIP ME WITH LOVE, I GIVE THE UNDERSTANDING BY WHICH THEY CAN COME TO ME.

OUT OF COMPASSION FOR THEM, I, DWELLING IN THEIR HEARTS, DESTROY WITH THE SHINING LAMP OF KNOWLEDGE THE DARKNESS BORN OF IGNORANCE.

Notes

Page 2	His Divine Grace A.C. Bhaktivedanta Swami Prabhupada
Page 5	Chapter 9, verse 2
Page 7	Chaitanya Mahaprabhu, the golden avatar, and his associates
Page 9	Chapter 2, verse 12
Page 11	Krishna instructing Arjuna in the science of *Bhagavad-gita*
Page 12	Sri Nathaji, the beloved deity of Nathdwar
Page 13	Chapter 2, verse 13
Page 15	Chapter 2, verse 20
Page 16	Garuda, the celestial carrier of Vishnu
Page 17	Vishnu, the Lord in the heart, the goal of the yogi
Page 18	Buddha, who appeared to mitigate the suffering of all living entities
Page 19	Chapter 2, verse 65
Page 21	Mother Yashoda and baby Krishna
Page 22	Vyasadeva, the compiler of the Vedas
Page 23	Chapter 4, verse 1
Page 25	Chapter 4, verse 3
Page 26-27	Krisna and Arjuna on the battlefield of Kurukshetra
Page 29	Chapter 4, verses 10, 15
Page 30	Saraswati, the goddess of learning
Page 31	Sri Narasimha, the wonderful incarnation
Page 33	Chapter 4, verse 34
Page 34	Ganesh, who removes impediments in the execution of devotional service

Page 35	Chapter 4, verse 36
Page 37	Krishna and His brother, Balaram, in the forest of Vrindavan
Page 38	Lord Shiva, Mahadeva
Page 39	Chapter 4, verse 38
Page 41	Rama, the incarnation of the Supreme as a perfect king, with Sita, Laksman, and Hanuman
Page 42	Hanuman, the monkey devotee who serves Lord Rama
Page 43	Chapter 5, verse 7
Page 44	Lord Brahma, the primeval living entity within the universe
Page 45	Chapter 5, verse 16
Page 46	Jaya Jaganatha!
Page 47	Chapter 5, verse 24
Page 49	Radha-Govinda enjoying their eternal pastimes
Page 50	Varaha, the incarnation of the Supreme as a giant boar
Page 51	Chapter 6, verses 5, 36
Page 53	Chapter 9, verse 26
Page 55	Krishna, the Cowherd Boy of Vrindavan
Page 57	Chapter 10, verses 10, 11
Page 58	Omkara—Om, the transcendental syllable which represents the Supreme
Page 59	Chapter 7, verse 6
Page 60	Sripad Sanatana Goswami Bhajan-kuti
Page 61	Chapter 10, verse 9
Page 62-63	Krishna and the cowherd boys
Page 65	Chapter 10, verses 39, 41
Page 67	The damsels of Vrajadhama, who manifested the highest love for Krishna
Page 69	Chapter 18, verses 61, 62
Page 71	Radha-Krishna, the Divine Couple
Page 72	Narada-Muni, the great sage and devotee of the Lord
Page 73	The Maha-mantra
Page 75	Krishna mandala

About the Authors

Kim Waters Murray is a painter and sculptor who has been inspired by the artistic and spiritual traditions of India. Her work has also been influenced by Medieval and Renaissance paintings, as well as Pre-Raphaelite and Celtic art.

Chris Murray is the director of Govinda Gallery in Washington, DC, and has organized over one hundred exhibitions of paintings, drawings and photographs. His love for India and its spiritual culture has led him to travel there frequently.

Kim and Chris' personal association with A.C. Bhaktivedanta Swami Prabhupada, the renowned Acarya (Sanskrit for spiritual master), inspired them to create *Illuminations From the Bhagavad-Gita*. Swami Bhaktivedanta's translation of the *Bhagavad-Gita As It Is* is the basis for *Illuminations*. The authors first met Srila Prabhupada, as he is affectionately known, in London in 1971. They continued to study with Srila Prabhupada in India and in the United States until his passing in 1977.

Chris and Kim have collaborated on a children's book, *The Butter Thief*, also published by the Mandala Publishing Group.